A Year of
Fat Bombs

INTRODUCTION

This idea was born from an email from a customer (thank you Nidza), which went something like this…

'Well, I normally fix meals to last me at most four serving or days. I'd plan to have a fat bomb every day.

That's 365 days divided by a recipe that makes at least a weeks' worth, so 52 recipes?

That's ideal. Are there 52 fat bomb recipes anywhere?

Perfection in my mind would be a seasonally adjusted book where you would split the recipes into four seasons.

To allow for not always sweet but savory recipes utilizing available produce and lots of fat. How's that for a crazy idea?'

And with this "crazy idea" in mind, I went about to create a range of fat bombs across the seasons. There is a good mixture of sweet and savory, along with some very special holiday-themed fat bombs.

This book was perhaps my most challenging and creative yet. So I hope you enjoy these fat bombs and they help you to stay keto by adding a bit of variety and delight to your diet.

As with most things… everything in moderation. Yes, they are ketogenic; however, I would not recommend getting all your daily calories from them. Use them as a treat, perhaps one a day as Nidza has suggested.

Elizabeth Jane

7

SPRING

21

SUMMER

FINAL NOTES
Adjusting and customizing the recipes

These recipes have been created to:

1. Be easy to make

2. Be delicious

3. Use easy to find ingredients

However, there is not a one-size-fits-all recipe, everyone has different tastes, some have allergies and not everyone will be able to get all of the ingredients. Consider the recipes as a guideline to which you can then customize to your taste or to what you have in the house.

- Love coconut? Try coconut flour instead of almond.
- Do not have any pink rock salt in the house? Just use some normal table salt instead.
- Do not like strawberries? Try blueberries.

I have included some suggestions throughout for alternatives, but could not list every single one.

Only you know what your preferences are, so have some fun with it and play around with different ingredients and recipes.

STORAGE

Most of the recipes are either stored in the refrigerator or the freezer. Keep them in an airtight container (particularly if in the refrigerator). If the stored frozen, I'd recommend consuming within 2 weeks, and if refrigerated, with 5-7 days. This may vary by recipe and I have included recipe specific recommendations if this is different.

And lastly, if you would be kind enough to leave an honest review, it would be most appreciated.

Please visit the below link:

http://ketojane.com/fatreview

Once again, thank you for buying and good luck!

Elizabeth Jane

KETO EASY MEALS BONUS SERIES

I am delighted you have chosen my book to help you start or continue on your keto journey. Keto meals can be hard, complicated ingredients, long cooking times… to help you stay on the keto track, I am pleased to offer you three mini ebooks from my 'Keto Easy Meals Bonus Series', completely free of charge! These three mini ebooks cover how to make everything from easy breakfasts, to 6 ingredient dinners and meals using just one pot (less prep and washing up)!

Simply visit the link below to get your free copy of all three mini ebooks:

http://ketojane.com/Bombbonus

SPRING

Red Valentines
Chocolate Coconut Bombs
Peanut Butter Explosion
Cream Cheese Craters
Savory Salmon Bites
Coconut Chocolate Fudge
Matcha And Dark Chocolate Cups
Limey Savory Pie
St. Patrick's Scrumptious Fudge
Fennel And Almond Bites
White Chocolate Bombs
Creamy Avocado & Bacon Balls
Macaroon

RED VALENTINES

Serves : 12
Preparation time : 5 minutes
Cooking time : None
Freezing time : 2 hours

ADDITIONAL TIP
If you don't have a piping bag or don't know how to operate one, then just get a flexible ice tray. Scoop the mixture into the ice compartments and freeze. You can get cute shapes for extra fun.

INGREDIENTS:

- 2 ounces half and half
- 4 diced strawberries
- 4 pitted cherries
- 4 tablespoons coconut oil
- 4 tablespoons grass-fed butter
- Stevia to taste

DIRECTIONS:

1. Add the diced strawberries and the cherries to a high-speed food processor. Pulse until pureed.

2. Add the half and half and Stevia. Blend so that everything is mixed well.

3. Melt the butter over a double boiler or in the microwave and add to the mixture. Also add the coconut oil and mix well.

4. Add the mixture to a piping bag. Squeeze out little droplets onto a baking tray and freeze for a few hours.

5. Keep stored in the freezer and enjoy as needed.

NUTRITION FACTS (PER SERVING)

Calories: 78   Fat: 9g   Protein: 0g   Total Carbohydrates: 1g   Dietary Fiber: 0g   Net Carbohydrates: 0g

CHOCOLATE COCONUT BOMBS

Serves	: 12
Preparation time	: 20 minutes
Cooking time	: None
Freezing time	: 1 hour

ADDITIONAL TIP
You can also add in about ½ cup shredded coconut for some texture.

INGREDIENTS:

- 1 cup coconut oil (solid)
- ½ cup dark cocoa powder
- 1 teaspoon peppermint extract
- ½ teaspoon vanilla extract
- 5 drops Stevia
- A pinch of salt

DIRECTIONS:

1. Add all the ingredients to a food processor and blend until combined.

2. Use a teaspoon to drop spoonfuls onto parchment paper.

3. Refrigerate until solidified and keep refrigerated.

NUTRITION FACTS (PER SERVING)

Calories: 126   Fat: 14g   Protein: 0g   Total Carbohydrates: 0g   Dietary Fiber: 0g   Net Carbohydrates: 0g

PEANUT BUTTER EXPLOSION

Serves : 12
Preparation time : 5 minutes
Cooking time : None
Freezing time : 2 hours

ADDITIONAL TIP
You can also use almond butter or hazelnut butter instead of peanut butter.

INGREDIENTS:

- ¼ cup peanut butter
- 2 tablespoons grass-fed butter
- 1 tablespoon coconut oil
- 2-3 drops Stevia
- ¼ cup crushed peanuts

DIRECTIONS:

1. Melt together the butter, peanut butter and coconut oil.

2. Stir in the sweetener. Form into balls and roll in the crushed nuts.

3. Drop into candy molds and place in the fridge for 2 hours.

NUTRITION FACTS (PER SERVING)

Calories: 58   Fat: 6g   Protein: 1g   Total Carbohydrates: 2g   Dietary Fiber: 0g   Net Carbohydrates: 2g

CREAM CHEESE CRATERS

Serves   : 12
Preparation time : 5 minutes
Cooking time   : None
Freezing time   : 3 hours

ADDITIONAL TIP
You can also use mascarpone cheese instead of cream cheese.

INGREDIENTS:

- ½ cup full-fat cream cheese
- ½ cup chopped walnuts or nuts of choice
- ½ cup grated dark chocolate
- Stevia to taste

FOR THE FILLING:

- 4 tablespoons grass-fed butter
- 2 tablespoons espresso powder
- 2 tablespoons heavy cream
- Stevia to taste

DIRECTIONS:

1. Soften the cream cheese and mix in the dark chocolate, chopped nuts and Stevia.

2. Take 12 mini cupcake liners and line the sides with the mixture so as to make a crater shape.

3. Place in the freezer for about 2 hours.

4. Meanwhile, melt the butter and whip in the heavy cream. Fold in rest of the filling ingredients.

5. Take the craters out of the freezer and fill each one with a small amount of filling.

6. Store in the refrigerator and enjoy whenever you like.

NUTRITION FACTS (PER SERVING)

Calories: 100   Fat: 10g   Protein: 2g   Total Carbohydrates: 2g   Dietary Fiber: 0g   Net Carbohydrates: 2g

SAVORY
SALMON BITES

Serves : 12   Preparation time : 5 minutes   Cooking time : None   Freezing time : None

INGREDIENTS:

- 50g smoked salmon trimmings
- 1 cup mascarpone cheese
- ⅔ cup grass-fed butter (softened)
- 1 tablespoon apple cider vinegar
- 1 tablespoon chopped parsley
- Salt to taste

DIRECTIONS:

1. Soften the cheese using a fork and mix in the vinegar, parsley and salt.

2. Add the butter and salmon trimmings and mix well.

3. Form into small balls and line on parchment paper.

4. Refrigerate until firm.

ADDITIONAL TIP
Try mackerel instead of salmon for a different taste.

NUTRITION FACTS (PER SERVING)

Calories: 117   Fat: 13g   Protein: 3g   Total Carbohydrates: 1g   Dietary Fiber: 0g   Net Carbohydrates: 1g

COCONUT
CHOCOLATE FUDGE

Serves : 12
Preparation time : 10 minutes
Cooking time : None
Freezing time : Overnight

ADDITIONAL TIP
Add in some chopped nuts for a nutty flavor.

INGREDIENTS:

- ⅓ cup dark chocolate chips
- ½ cup cocoa powder
- ½ cup coconut oil
- ¼ cup full-fat coconut milk
- 1 teaspoon vanilla extract
- Stevia to taste

DIRECTIONS:

1. Melt the coconut oil and add to a blender.
2. Add in the rest of the ingredients and blend until smooth and creamy.
3. Line a bread pan with parchment paper and pour in the mixture.
4. Freeze overnight.
5. Cut into small squares and store in the refrigerator.

NUTRITION FACTS (PER SERVING)

Calories: 78   Fat: 8g   Protein: 1g   Total Carbohydrates: 4g   Dietary Fiber: 1g   Net Carbohydrates: 3g

MATCHA
& DARK CHOCOLATE CUPS

Serves : 12   Preparation time : 10 minutes   Cooking time : None   Freezing time : 2 hours

INGREDIENTS:

- 10 ounces dark chocolate chips
- ¼ cup grass-fed butter
- ½ tablespoon matcha green tea powder
- 2 teaspoons coconut oil
- Stevia to taste

DIRECTIONS:

1. Melt the chocolate chips over a double boiler and stir in the coconut oil.

2. Grease or line a muffin tray and brush the chocolate mixture onto the sides.

3. Transfer to a freezer for about an hour.

4. Meanwhile, soften the butter and mix in the matcha powder and Stevia.

5. When the crusts of the cups are set, remove from the freezer and scoop in the matcha mixture.

6. Store in the refrigerator and use as needed.

ADDITIONAL TIP
You can add more matcha powder if you want a stronger flavor.

NUTRITION FACTS (PER SERVING)

Calories: 135   Fat: 14g   Protein: 1g   Total Carbohydrates: 3g   Dietary Fiber: 2g   Net Carbohydrates: 1g

LIMEY SAVORY PIE

Serves : 12
Preparation time : 5 minutes
Cooking time : 7 minutes
Freezing time : 2 hours

ADDITIONAL TIP
I personally like a cheeky drizzle of melted dark chocolate on top. It complements the lime well.

INGREDIENTS:

- 1 cup almond flour
- 3 tablespoons butter
- 1 tablespoon ground cinnamon
- ½ teaspoon vanilla extract
- Stevia to taste

FOR THE FILLING:

- 4 ounces full-fat cream cheese
- ¼ cup coconut oil
- 3 tablespoons grass-fed butter
- 2 limes
- Stevia to taste
- A handful of baby spinach (optional – adds color)

DIRECTIONS:

1. Mix the first five ingredients to form a crumble mixture.

2. Press this mixture into the bottom of 12 muffin cups and bake for 7 minutes at 350 degrees.

3. While the crusts are baking, juice the lime and grate for zest.

4. Add all the filling ingredients to a food processor and blend until smooth.

5. Cool the crusts to room temperature and then pour this mixture in the center. Freeze until set.

NUTRITION FACTS (PER SERVING)

Calories: 146   Fat: 15g   Protein: 3g   Total Carbohydrates: 2g   Dietary Fiber: 1g   Net Carbohydrates: 1g

ST. PATRICK'S SCRUMPTIOUS FUDGE

Serves   : 12
Preparation time : 10 minutes
Cooking time   : None
Freezing time   : Overnight

ADDITIONAL TIP
1. Use shamrock-shaped molds for a fun presentation.
2. Include some ground nuts for a different taste.

INGREDIENTS:

- 10 ounces coconut oil
- 4 tablespoons cocoa powder
- 2 tablespoons granulated Stevia
- ½ teaspoon peppermint extract

DIRECTIONS:

1. Combine all the ingredients and mix well.

2. Pour into molds or ice trays and refrigerate overnight.

3. Voila! Easy and delicious fat bombs are ready.

NUTRITION FACTS (PER SERVING)

Calories: 206   Fat: 24g   Protein: 0g   Total Carbohydrates: 0g   Dietary Fiber: 0g   Net Carbohydrates: 0g

FENNEL
& ALMOND BITES

Serves : 12   Preparation time : 5 minutes   Cooking time : None   Freezing time : 3 hours

INGREDIENTS:

- ¼ cup almond milk
- ¼ cup almond oil
- ¼ cup cacao powder
- 1 teaspoon fennel seeds
- 1 teaspoon vanilla extract (optional)
- A pinch of salt

DIRECTIONS:

1. Mix the almond milk and almond oil and beat until smooth and glossy. Use an electric beater for quicker results.
2. Mix in rest of the ingredients.
3. Pour into a piping bag and get creative with the shapes. Make sure to use parchment paper as a base or they might stick.
4. Freeze for 3 hours and then keep stored in the refrigerator.

ADDITIONAL TIP
You can also use coconut milk and coconut oil instead of almond.

NUTRITION FACTS (PER SERVING)

Calories: 172   Fat: 20g   Protein: 1g   Total Carbohydrates: 1g   Dietary Fiber: 1g   Net Carbohydrates: 0g

WHITE CHOCOLATE BOMBS

Serves : 12
Preparation time : 15 minutes
Cooking time : 5 minutes
Freezing time : 1 hour

ADDITIONAL TIP
Try different types of chocolate to create a great variety of bombs!

INGREDIENTS:

- 4 ounces cocoa butter
- 1 ½ cups chopped pecans or walnuts
- 6 tablespoons grass-fed butter
- 6 tablespoons coconut oil
- ¾ teaspoon vanilla extract
- ⅛ teaspoon sea salt
- Stevia to taste

CHOCOLATE COATING:

- ¼ ounce cocoa butter
- 1 ounce white baking chocolate, unsweetened
- ⅛ teaspoon stevia extract
- ⅛ teaspoon vanilla extract

DIRECTIONS:

1. Melt the butter, cocoa powder and coconut oil over a double boiler. Mix well.

2. Add in the rest of the (non-chocolate coating) ingredients and combine.

3. Pour into your favorite molds/cupcake pan and place in the refrigerator overnight.

4. To prepare the white chocolate coating, melt the chocolate and butter over a double broiler and add in the vanilla and stevia.

5. Remove the base from the molds and dip in the chocolate coating. Then leave in the fridge for 2-3 hours to set.

NUTRITION FACTS (PER SERVING)

Calories: 287   Fat: 30g   Protein: 1g   Total Carbohydrates: Less than 1g   Dietary Fiber: 0g
Net Carbohydrates: Less than 1g

CREAMY
AVOCADO & BACON·BALLS

Serves : 12   Preparation time : 10 minutes   Cooking time : 15 minutes   Freezing time : None

INGREDIENTS:

- 1 avocado
- 1 chili pepper
- 1 onion
- ½ cup grass-fed butter
- 4 bacon slices
- 1 tablespoon fresh lime juice
- ¼ teaspoon sea salt
- A pinch of pepper

DIRECTIONS:

1. Chop the onions and chili peppers (deseed if you prefer it a bit milder).
2. Fry the bacon in its grease until crispy.
3. Cut and dice the avocado.
4. Add all the ingredients, including the bacon grease (not the bacon itself), to a food processor and blend until smooth.
5. Chop the bacon and mix with the creamy mixture.
6. Drop spoonfuls onto parchment paper.
7. Refrigerate for 2-3 hours.
8. Serve when firm.

ADDITIONAL TIP
If you are not a fan of spicy food, either use a mild chili pepper or leave it out altogether.

NUTRITION FACTS (PER SERVING)

Calories: 156   Fat: 15g   Protein: 3g   Total Carbohydrates: 3g   Dietary Fiber: 1g   Net Carbohydrates: 1g

MACAROONS

Serves : 12   Preparation time : 10 minutes   Cooking time : 15 minutes   Freezing time : None

INGREDIENTS:

- ½ cup coconut flakes
- ¼ cup almond meal
- 1 tablespoon coconut oil
- 1 teaspoon vanilla extract
- 3 egg whites
- Stevia to taste

DIRECTIONS:

1. Sift together all the dry ingredients.
2. Melt coconut oil and stir in the vanilla extract.
3. Pour the coconut oil into the dry mixture and mix well.
4. Beat the egg whites until stiff peaks form.
5. Fold into the other mixture.
6. Drop spoonfuls onto a baking tray lined with parchment paper.
7. Bake for 8 minutes at 400 degrees.
8. Cool and enjoy!

ADDITIONAL TIP
If you have trouble getting the egg whites to form stiff peaks, use a chilled bowl and lots of patience.

NUTRITION FACTS (PER SERVING)

Calories: 46   Fat: 5g   Protein: 2g   Total Carbohydrates: Less than 1g   Dietary Fiber: 0g
Net Carbohydrates: Less than 1g

SUMMER

Tangy Coco Bombs
Mascarpone Mocha Fat Bombs
Tropical Truffles
Pepperoni Pizza Pastries
Chives And Cheese
Jell-O Fat Bombs
Berry Cheese Nut Ball
Mini Strawberry Cheesecakes
Ice Cream Fat Bombs
Blueberry Bombs
Zingy Lemon Bombs
Tiny Spicy Explosions
Cheesy Garlic Fat Bombs

TANGY COCO BOMBS

Serves : 12
Preparation time : 5 minutes
Cooking time : None
Freezing time : 3 hours

ADDITIONAL TIP

If the cream cheese separates during mixing (might happen due to the tartness of limes), don't worry. Your fat bombs will still turn out awesome.

INGREDIENTS:

- 2 ounces full-fat cream cheese
- ½ ounce coconut flakes
- ¼ cup grass-fed butter
- ½ cup coconut oil
- 2 tablespoons coconut cream
- 2 teaspoons vanilla extract
- 2 limes
- Stevia to taste

DIRECTIONS:

1. Juice the limes and grate for zest.

2. Melt together the butter and coconut oil.

3. Remove from heat and mix in the coconut cream and cream cheese. Mix well.

4. Add in the rest of the ingredients (except the coconut flakes) and mix well.

5. Roll into small balls and roll in the coconut flakes so they receive a good coating.

6. Place into either molds or cupcake pan and freeze.

NUTRITION FACTS (PER SERVING)

Calories: 122   Fat: 14g   Protein: 1g   Total Carbohydrates: 1g   Dietary Fiber: 0g   Net Carbohydrates:1g

MASCARPONE
MOCHA FAT BOMBS

Serves : 12
Preparation time : 10 minutes
Cooking time : None
Freezing time : 3 hours

ADDITIONAL TIP
You can also mix by hand but it will take much longer.

INGREDIENTS:

- ½ cup mascarpone cheese
- 3 tablespoons granulated Stevia
- 2 tablespoons grass-fed butter
- 1 tablespoon coconut oil
- 1 ½ tablespoon cacao powder, divided
- ½ teaspoon rum (optional)
- ¼ teaspoon instant coffee
- More Stevia to taste

DIRECTIONS:

1. Add all the ingredients (reserve ½ tablespoon cacao powder) to a blender and pulse until consistency is smooth and creamy.

2. Pour into silicone molds and sprinkle the remaining cacao powder on top. Freeze and enjoy.

NUTRITION FACTS (PER SERVING)

Calories: 77   Fat: 8g   Protein: 1g   Total Carbohydrates: 1g   Dietary Fiber: 0g   Net Carbohydrates: 1g

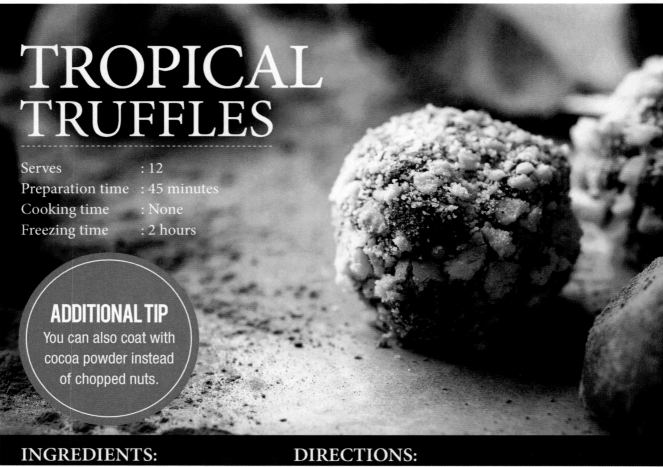

TROPICAL TRUFFLES

Serves   : 12
Preparation time : 45 minutes
Cooking time   : None
Freezing time   : 2 hours

ADDITIONAL TIP
You can also coat with cocoa powder instead of chopped nuts.

INGREDIENTS:

- ⅔ cup protein powder (any flavor)
- ¼ cup coconut milk
- ¼ cup white chocolate chips
- 4 tablespoons coconut flakes
- 4 tablespoons coconut oil

FOR THE TOPPING:

- ⅔ cup coconut butter
- 3 tablespoons chopped nuts
- 1 teaspoon coconut oil

DIRECTIONS:

1. Mix the non-topping ingredients until it is thoroughly combined and pour into molds. Freeze until the base is set. This will typically take an hour.

2. Meanwhile, melt together the coconut butter and coconut oil.

3. Dip each frozen truffle in the mixture and sprinkle with chopped nuts.

4. Return to the freezer for another half an hour (or store in the fridge) and enjoy!

NUTRITION FACTS (PER SERVING)

Calories: 249   Fat: 26g   Protein: 5g   Total Carbohydrates: 2g   Dietary Fiber: 1g   Net Carbohydrates: 1g

PEPPERONI
PIZZA PASTRIES

Serves : 12   Preparation time : 20 minutes   Cooking time : None   Freezing time : None

INGREDIENTS:

- 14 beef pepperoni slices
- 8 button mushrooms
- 8 pitted olives
- 4 ounces mascarpone cheese
- 2 tablespoons pesto
- 2 tablespoons chopped basil
- Salt and pepper to taste

DIRECTIONS:

1. Slice the pepperoni, olives and mushrooms into small pieces.
2. Sauté the mushrooms in a pan for 2-3 minutes, until brown. Then allow to cool.
3. In a bowl, combine the cheese, pesto, salt and pepper.
4. Add the olives, mushrooms, pepperoni and basil. Mix well.
5. Form into small balls and serve. No need to freeze or cook.

ADDITIONAL TIP
Get creative and add as many toppings as you like.

NUTRITION FACTS (PER SERVING)

Calories: 110   Fat: 11g   Protein: 2g   Total Carbohydrates: 2g   Dietary Fiber: 0g   Net Carbohydrates: 2g

CHIVES & CHEESE

Serves : 12
Preparation time : 5 minutes
Cooking time : None
Freezing time : None

ADDITIONAL TIP
Stack together with cherry tomatoes to make a great starter

INGREDIENTS:

- 2 ½ ounces full-fat cream cheese
- ¼ cup fresh chives
- Salt to taste
- Almond flour

DIRECTIONS:

1. Thinly chop the chives.

2. Soften the cream cheese and mix it together with the chives and salt. Add almond flour to adjust the consistency.

3. Form into small balls and chill for about 30 minutes in the refrigerator.

NUTRITION FACTS (PER SERVING)

Calories: 38   Fat: 3g   Protein: 7g   Total Carbohydrates: Less than 1g   Dietary Fiber: 0g
Net Carbohydrates: Less than 1g

JELL-O
FAT BOMBS

Serves : 12   Preparation time : 10 minutes   Cooking time : None   Freezing time : 2 hours

INGREDIENTS:

- 8 ounces full-fat cream cheese
- 1 pack Jell-O (any flavor and sugar-free)
- 1 teaspoon lemon juice

DIRECTIONS:

1. Soften the cream cheese and mix in the lemon juice.
2. Form into small balls.
3. Roll in Jell-O and place in the fridge overnight.

ADDITIONAL TIP
Add some chopped fruit of the same flavor as the Jell-O for extra fruity goodness.

NUTRITION FACTS (PER SERVING)

Calories: 105   Fat: 9g   Protein: 3g   Total Carbohydrates: 1g   Dietary Fiber: 0g   Net Carbohydrates: 1g

BERRY CHEESE
NUT BALLS

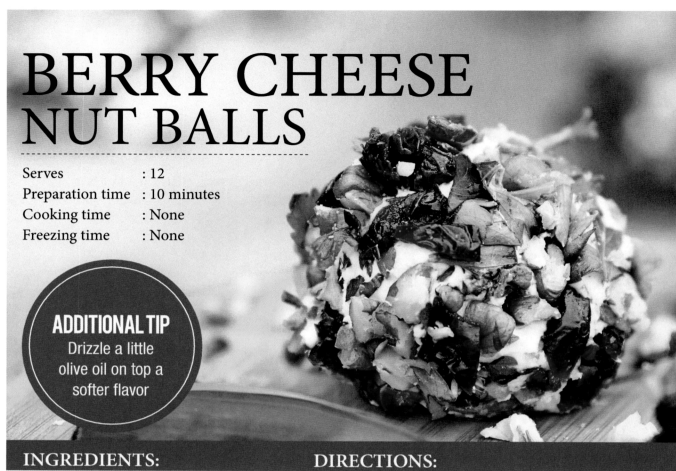

Serves   : 12
Preparation time : 10 minutes
Cooking time   : None
Freezing time   : None

ADDITIONAL TIP
Drizzle a little olive oil on top a softer flavor

INGREDIENTS:

- 6 ounces goat cheese
- ⅔ cup dried cranberries
- ¼ cup chopped pecans
- 2 tablespoons chopped parsley
- Salt to taste

DIRECTIONS:

1. Chop the cranberries into small pieces.
2. Soften the cheese and mix together all the ingredients.
3. Form into small balls and chill for about 45 minutes
4. Serve and enjoy!

NUTRITION FACTS (PER SERVING)

Calories: 125   Fat: 10g   Protein: 7g   Total Carbohydrates: 3g   Dietary Fiber: 1g   Net Carbohydrates: 2g

MINI STRAWBERRY CHEESECAKES

Serves : 12   Preparation time : 10 minutes   Cooking time : None   Freezing time : 2-3 hours

INGREDIENTS:

- 1 cup coconut butter
- 1 cup coconut oil
- ½ cup sliced strawberries
- 2 tablespoons full-fat cream cheese
- ½ teaspoon lime juice
- Stevia to taste

DIRECTIONS:

1. Add the strawberries to a food processor and puree.

2. Soften the cream cheese and coconut butter.

3. Combine all the ingredients.

4. Add to silicone molds and freeze for about 2 hours. Keep stored in the refrigerator.

ADDITIONAL TIP
try raspberries or blackberries instead of strawberries.

NUTRITION FACTS (PER SERVING)

Calories: 372   Fat: 41g   Protein: 1g   Total Carbohydrates: 3g   Dietary Fiber: 1g   Net Carbohydrates: 2g

ICE CREAM
FAT BOMBS

Serves : 12   Preparation time : 10 minutes   Cooking time : None   Freezing time : 2 hours

INGREDIENTS:

- 3 cups protein powder of your favorite ice cream flavor
- 1 cup cashew butter
- 1 cup whipped cream
- Stevia to taste

DIRECTIONS:

1. Place the whipped cream in a bowl and gently fold in protein powder, Stevia, and cashew butter.

2. Pour the mixture in silicone molds and freeze.

3. Enjoy the frozen dessert.

ADDITIONAL TIP
Top with some chopped berries or sugar-free syrup

NUTRITION FACTS (PER SERVING)

Calories: 250   Fat: 19g   Protein: 11g   Total Carbohydrates: 10g   Dietary Fiber: 2g   Net Carbohydrates: 8g

BLUEBERRY BOMBS

Serves : 12
Preparation time : 15 minutes
Cooking time : None
Freezing time : 3-4 hours

ADDITIONAL TIP
The berries do not have to be blue-try your favorite berries instead.

INGREDIENTS:

- 2 tablespoons almond butter
- 1 tablespoon coconut oil
- 1 tablespoon cacao powder
- ¼ teaspoon ground cinnamon
- Stevia to taste
- A pinch of salt

FOR THE TOPPING:

- ¼ cup grass-fed butter
- ¼ cup cream cheese
- ¼ cup pureed blueberries
- 1 tablespoon heavy whipping creams
- 1 teaspoon vanilla extract

DIRECTIONS:

1. Combine the non-topping ingredients in a bowl to form an even mixture.

2. Spread in a bread pan lined with parchment paper. Freeze until set.

3. In the meantime, add the topping ingredients to a blender and whirl to whip them up.

4. Remove the base from freezer and cut into squares. Spread the topping on each square and return to the freezer.

NUTRITION FACTS (PER SERVING)

Calories: 77   Fat: 8g   Protein: 1g   Total Carbohydrates: 1g   Dietary Fiber: 0g   Net Carbohydrates: 1g

ZINGY
LEMON BOMBS

Serves   : 12
Preparation time : 5 minutes
Cooking time   : None
Freezing time   : 2 hours

ADDITIONAL TIP
You can also pop them onto sticks like lolli-pops. All you have to do is stick a wooden skewer into each mold

INGREDIENTS:

- 4 ounces cream cheese
- ¼ cup grass-fed butter
- ¼ cup coconut oil
- 3-4 lemons
- Stevia to taste
- Yellow food coloring (optional)

DIRECTIONS:

1. Juice the lemons and grate for zest.

2. Add all the ingredients to a food processor and mix well.

3. Pour into molds and freeze until set.

NUTRITION FACTS (PER SERVING)

Calories: 75   Fat: 8g   Protein: 2g   Total Carbohydrates: 1g   Dietary Fiber: 0g   Net Carbohydrates: 1g

TINY SPICY EXPLOSIONS

Serves : 12   Preparation time : 25 minutes   Cooking time : None   Freezing time : None

INGREDIENTS:

- 12 ounces cream cheese
- 3 jalapeno peppers
- 12 bacon slices
- 1 ½ teaspoons dried parsley
- ¾ teaspoon garlic powder
- ¾ teaspoon onion powder
- ¼ teaspoon kosher salt
- Pepper to taste

DIRECTIONS:

1. Fry the bacon until crispy and chop into tiny pieces.

2. Slice the jalapeno peppers thinly.

3. Soften the cream cheese and combine all the ingredients (including bacon and jalapenos).

4. Form into small balls and chill for about 30 minutes.

5. Serve with a dip of choice.

ADDITIONAL TIP
Don't waste the bacon grease. Add it to the mix as well.

NUTRITION FACTS (PER SERVING)

Calories: 207   Fat: 19g   Protein: 5g   Total Carbohydrates: 2g   Dietary Fiber: 1g   Net Carbohydrates: 1g

CHEESY GARLIC FAT BOMBS

Serves	: 12
Preparation time	: 7-10 minutes
Cooking time	: None
Freezing time	: None

ADDITIONAL TIP
You can also add in some chopped vegetables if you like.

INGREDIENTS:

- 4 cups shredded mozzarella cheese
- 1 cup keto crumbs
- 4 tablespoons grass-fed butter
- 2 teaspoons garlic paste
- 2 teaspoons cilantro paste
- Salt to taste

DIRECTIONS:

1. Mix all the ingredients. The consistency will be dough-like.

2. Using your hands, make into small irregular shapes. It will be difficult to get them to form balls.

3. Roll in keto crumbs and lay on parchment paper.

4. Refrigerate until firm (about 1-2 hours).

5. Serve with a dip of choice.

NUTRITION FACTS (PER SERVING)

Calories: 141   Fat: 11g   Protein: 9g   Total Carbohydrates: 1g   Dietary Fiber: 0g   Net Carbohydrates: 1g

FALL

ALMOND DELIGHTS

Serves	: 12
Preparation time	: 10 minutes
Cooking time	: None
Freezing time	: 2 hours

ADDITIONAL TIP

I suggest melting butter over a double boiler because direct melting can scald and burn the butter, hence ruining the taste. Try adding in some chopped almonds for some added texture

INGREDIENTS:

- 18 ounces grass-fed butter
- 2 ounces heavy cream
- ⅔ cup cocoa powder
- ½ cup granulated Stevia
- 4 tablespoons almond butter
- 1 teaspoon vanilla extract

DIRECTIONS:

1. Melt the butter over a double boiler.
2. Add in the rest of the ingredients and mix well.
3. Place into your favorite molds and freeze for 2 hours.

NUTRITION FACTS (PER SERVING)

Calories: 350   Fat: 38g   Protein: 2g   Total Carbohydrates: 4g   Dietary Fiber: 2g   Net Carbohydrates: 0g

SALTED CARAMEL CONES

Serves : 12   Preparation time : 5 minutes   Cooking time : None   Freezing time : 2 hours

INGREDIENTS:

- ⅓ cup coconut oil
- ⅓ cup grass-fed butter
- 2 tablespoons heavy whipping cream
- 2 tablespoons sour cream
- 1 tablespoon caramel sugar
- 1 teaspoon sea salt
- Stevia to taste

DIRECTIONS:

1. Soften the butter and coconut oil.
2. Mix all the ingredients to form a batter.
3. Pour into a cone or triangle shaped molds. Freeze until they set.
4. Sprinkle with a little more salt on top and enjoy!
5. Store in the fridge.

ADDITIONAL TIP
Don't use regular table salt. Use a more coarse salt like kosher or sea salt, which gives the best texture and flavor.

NUTRITION FACTS (PER SERVING)

Calories: 100   Fat: 12g   Protein: 0g   Total Carbohydrates: 1g   Dietary Fiber: 0g   Net Carbohydrates: 1g

MINI
CINNAMON BUNS

Serves : 12   Preparation time : 5 minutes   Cooking time : None   Freezing time : 2 hours

INGREDIENTS:

- 8 ounces cream cheese
- ½ cup grass-fed butter
- 4 tablespoons coconut oil
- 1 teaspoon vanilla extract
- ¼ teaspoon ground cinnamon
- ⅛ teaspoon ground nutmeg
- Stevia to taste

DIRECTIONS:

1. Soften the butter and coconut oil. Mix in the cream cheese.

2. Add in the rest of the ingredients and mix until homogenous.

3. Pour into silicone molds and freeze until set.

ADDITIONAL TIP
Drizzle a little sugar-free caramel syrup on top.

NUTRITION FACTS (PER SERVING)

Calories: 165   Fat: 18g   Protein: 1g   Total Carbohydrates: 1g   Dietary Fiber: 0g   Net Carbohydrates: 1g

CHAI BITES

Serves : 12   Preparation time : 5 minutes   Cooking time : None   Freezing time : 2 hours

INGREDIENTS:

- 1 cup cream cheese
- 1 cup coconut oil
- 2 ounces grass-fed butter
- 2 teaspoons ground ginger
- 2 teaspoons ground cardamom
- 1 teaspoon ground nutmeg
- 1 teaspoon ground cloves
- 1 teaspoon Darjeeling black tea
- 1 teaspoon vanilla extract
- Stevia to taste

DIRECTIONS:

1. Melt the butter and coconut oil in a saucepan and add the black tea. Wait for it to color the mixture.
2. Add in cream cheese and remove from heat. Stir well.
3. Add in all the spices and stir to make a batter.
4. Pour into silicon molds and freeze until they set.
5. Enjoy with some actual tea or in the evenings in place of tea.
6. Store in the refrigerator.

NUTRITION FACTS (PER SERVING)

Calories: 178   Fat: 19g   Protein: 1g   Total Carbohydrates: 1g   Dietary Fiber: 0g   Net Carbohydrates: 1g

MAPLE & PECAN BARS

Serves : 12
Preparation time : 10 minutes
Cooking time : 25 minutes
Freezing time : None

ADDITIONAL TIP
Since they are baked, they can be stored in an airtight jar at room temperature for up to a week.

INGREDIENTS:

- 2 cups chopped pecans
- 1 cup almond meal
- ½ cup sugar-free chocolate chips
- ½ cup flaxseed meal
- ½ cup coconut oil (heat slightly to become liquid)
- ½ cup sugar-free maple syrup
- 20-25 drops Stevia

DIRECTIONS:

1. Spread the pecans in a baking dish and bake at 350 degrees until aromatic (will usually take from 6 to 8 minutes).

2. In the meanwhile, sift together all the dry ingredients.

3. Add the roasted pecans to the mix and mix well.

4. Add the maple syrup and coconut oil and stir to make a thick, sticky mixture.

5. Pour in a bread pan lined with parchment paper.

6. Bake for about 18 minutes at 350°F or until the top has browned.

7. Slice and enjoy!

NUTRITION FACTS (PER SERVING)

Calories: 302   Fat: 30g   Protein: 5g   Total Carbohydrates: 6g   Dietary Fiber: 4g   Net Carbohydrates: 2g

PUMPKIN
PIE FAT BOMBS

Serves : 12   Preparation time : 35 minutes   Cooking time : 5 minutes   Freezing time : 3 hours

INGREDIENTS:

- ⅓ cup pumpkin puree
- ⅓ cup almond butter
- ¼ cup almond oil
- 3 ounces sugar-free dark chocolate
- 2 tablespoons coconut oil
- 1 ½ teaspoon pumpkin pie spice mix
- Stevia to taste

DIRECTIONS:

1. Melt dark chocolate and almond oil over a double boiler.

2. Layer the bottom of 12 muffin cups with this mixture and freeze until the crust has set.

3. Meanwhile, combine the rest of the ingredients in a saucepan and put on low heat.

4. Heat until softened and mix well.

5. Pour this over the initial chocolate mixture and chill for at least 1 hour.

ADDITIONAL TIP
Use pumpkin puree without any added ingredients.

NUTRITION FACTS (PER SERVING)

Calories: 124   Fat: 13g   Protein: 3g   Total Carbohydrates: 3g   Dietary Fiber: 1g   Net Carbohydrates: 2g

CHOCO-PB EXPLOSIONS

Serves : 12
Preparation time : 12 minutes
Cooking time : 20 minutes
Freezing time : None

INGREDIENTS:

- 2 cups almond flour
- ⅓ cup crunchy peanut butter
- ¼ cup coconut oil (heat gently so it is liquid)
- 4 ounce dark chocolate bar (sugar free)
- 3 tablespoon sugar-free maple syrup
- 1 tablespoon vanilla extract
- 1 ¼ teaspoon baking powder
- A pinch of salt

DIRECTIONS:

1. In a large bowl, whisk together all the wet ingredients. The mixture will be light brown.
2. In another bowl, mix all the dry ingredients except the chocolate.
3. Now sift dry ingredients into the wet ingredients while continuing to mix. You want the batter to be smooth and not lumpy.
4. A crumbly mixture will form. Form this crumbly mixture into a ball and wrap it in cling film. Refrigerate for about an hour.
5. While the ball is in the fridge, cut up chocolate into small 1-inch pieces.
6. Take out dough from the fridge and make small balls. Place a piece of chocolate in the middle of each ball.
7. Line on a baking tray.
8. Bake for about 18 minutes at 350°F.
9. Sprinkle with some ground cinnamon, cool and enjoy!

NUTRITION FACTS (PER SERVING)

Calories: 148   Fat: 13g   Protein: 4g   Total Carbohydrates: 4g   Dietary Fiber: 2g   Net Carbohydrates: 2g

COCOA-COATED BACON BOMBS

Serves : 12
Preparation time : 10 minutes
Cooking time : 50 minutes
Freezing time : None

ADDITIONAL TIP
You can also fry the bacon instead of baking.

INGREDIENTS:

- 12 bacon slices
- 1 tablespoon sugar-free maple syrup
- Granulated Stevia to taste

FOR THE COATING:

- ¼ cup chopped pecans
- 4 tablespoons dark cocoa powder
- 15-20 drops Stevia

DIRECTIONS:

1. Lay the bacon slices on a baking tray and rub with maple syrup and Stevia. Flip the slices and do the same with the other side.

2. Bake for 10-15 minutes at 275°F (until crispy).

3. When done, drain the bacon grease.

4. Mix the bacon grease, cocoa powder and Stevia to form a batter.

5. Dip the bacon slices in the batter, roll in chopped pecans and allow to air dry until the chocolate hardens.

NUTRITION FACTS (PER SERVING)

Calories: 157   Fat: 11g Protein: 10g   Total Carbohydrates: 1g   Dietary Fiber: 0g   Net Carbohydrates: 1g

NUTTY NOUGATS

Serves	: 12
Preparation time	: 5 minutes
Cooking time	: 5 minutes
Freezing time	: 1 hour

ADDITIONAL TIP
Don't like the nuts listed? Use whatever nuts you like.

INGREDIENTS:

- 4 ounces cocoa butter
- 2 ounces chopped macadamia nuts
- 2 ounces chopped walnuts
- 2 ounces chopped pecans
- 1 cup heavy cream
- 2 tablespoons cocoa powder
- Stevia to taste

DIRECTIONS:

1. Melt the cocoa butter over a double boiler. Gradually stir in cocoa powder and Stevia.

2. Mix well. Remove from heat.

3. Whisk in heavy cream and fold all the nuts in.

4. Pour into molds and refrigerate until set.

NUTRITION FACTS (PER SERVING)

Calories: 367   Fat: 28g   Protein: 3g   Total Carbohydrates: 3g   Dietary Fiber: 0g   Net Carbohydrates: 3g

FRIED FRESCO CHEESE

Serves	: 12
Preparation time	: 2 minutes
Cooking time	: 5-7 minutes
Freezing time	: None

ADDITIONAL TIP
You can also add various spices to enhance the flavor.

INGREDIENTS:

- 2 pounds queso fresco
- 2 tablespoons coconut oil
- 1 tablespoon olive oil
- 1 tablespoon chopped basil

DIRECTIONS:

1. Heat together coconut and olive oil in a pan.
2. Cut the cheese into small cubes.
3. Fry in oil. Make sure to fry all sides until brown.
4. Sprinkle with fresh basil and enjoy!

NUTRITION FACTS (PER SERVING)

Calories: 243   Fat: 19g   Protein: 16g   Total Carbohydrates: 0g   Dietary Fiber: 0g   Net Carbohydrates: 0g

APPLE ROUNDS

Serves : 12   Preparation time : 5 minutes   Cooking time : 5 minutes   Freezing time : 3 hours

INGREDIENTS:

- 2 medium-sized apples
- 5 ounces heavy cream
- ½ cup grass-fed butter
- 2 tablespoons coconut oil
- 1 teaspoon ground cinnamon
- Stevia to taste
- A pinch of salt

DIRECTIONS:

1. Thinly slice the apples.
2. Melt the coconut oil in a pan and add in the apples and cinnamon. Mix well to coat the apples.
3. Cook until they become tender. Softly mash them with your spoon.
4. Remove from heat and fold in rest of the ingredients.
5. Pour into candy molds (preferably apple shaped) and freeze for about 3 hours.
6. Store in the refrigerator.

ADDITIONAL TIP
Apples are relatively high in carbohydrates, so use these as an occasional treat

NUTRITION FACTS (PER SERVING)

Calories: 168   Fat: 12g   Protein: 0g   Total Carbohydrates: 10g   Dietary Fiber: 2g   Net Carbohydrates: 8g

CREAM CHEESE CLOUDS

Serves	: 5 minutes
Preparation time	: None
Cooking time	: 12
Freezing time	: 1 hour

ADDITIONAL TIP
You can also different flavored extracts (e.g. orange, peppermint etc.) to make a variety of flavors.

INGREDIENTS:

- ½ cup grass-fed butter
- 8 ounces cream cheese
- ½ teaspoon vanilla extract
- Stevia to taste

DIRECTIONS:

1. Whisk everything together using an electric beater until frothy.
2. Drop spoonfuls onto a tray and freeze until set.

NUTRITION FACTS (PER SERVING)

Calories: 134   Fat: 14g   Protein: 1g   Total Carbohydrates: 1g   Dietary Fiber: 1g   Net Carbohydrates: 0g

SPICY PUMPKIN FAT BOMBS

Serves	: 12
Preparation time	: 10 minutes
Cooking time	: 6 minutes
Freezing time	: Overnight

ADDITIONAL TIP

A really fun thing that you can do is that you can add a few of these bombs (or the pre-frozen mixture) to a food processor and blend with some coconut or regular dairy milk to get an instant pumpkin smoothie. Add some instant coffee for a quick latte

INGREDIENTS:

- ½ cup diced pumpkin
- 3 tablespoons coconut butter
- 1 ½ tablespoons coconut oil
- ¼ teaspoon ground ginger
- ¼ teaspoon ground nutmeg
- ¼ teaspoon ground cinnamon
- ⅛ teaspoon ground cloves
- Stevia to taste

DIRECTIONS:

1. Melt the coconut oil and add it to the coconut butter. Add in Stevia and whisk until smooth.

2. Add the diced pumpkin and the spices to a food processor and pulse to roughly chop them up into very small pieces.

3. Mix the two together and stir well.

4. Make into small balls and line on a piece of parchment paper.

5. Place in the fridge and allow to set.

NUTRITION FACTS (PER SERVING)

Calories: 99   Fat: 10g   Protein: 2g   Total Carbohydrates: 1g   Dietary Fiber: 0g   Net Carbohydrates: 1g

WINTER

Breakfast Bacon Bombs

Creamy Coconut Fudge

Nutmeg Nougats

Cocoa Brownie

Orange Oodles

Mini Minty Happiness

Cheddar Cupcake

Seed-Filled Bombs

Nutty Ginger Bombs

Custard Cups

Nutty White Chocolate Truffles

Warm And Fluffy Fat Bombs

Cheese-Centered Bacon Balls

BREAKFAST
BACON BOMBS

Serves : 12   Preparation time : 10 minutes   Cooking time : 15 minutes   Freezing time : 1 hour

INGREDIENTS:

- 8 bacon slices
- 4 eggs
- ⅔ cup grass-fed butter
- 2 tablespoons full-fat keto-friendly mayonnaise
- 1 tablespoon chopped cilantro
- ¼ teaspoon cayenne pepper
- Salt and pepper to taste

DIRECTIONS:

1. Hard boil the eggs.

2. While the eggs are boiling, fry the bacon until crispy. Reserve the bacon grease.

3. When done, peel the eggs and mash them with a fork. Mix in butter, mayonnaise and seasonings.

4. Crumble the bacon into small pieces and mix into the main mixture.

5. Refrigerate for at least an hour.

6. Form into small balls and return to the fridge.

ADDITIONAL TIP
Customize the seasonings to your liking.

NUTRITION FACTS (PER SERVING)

Calories: 185   Fat: 18g   Protein: 5g   Total Carbohydrates: 0g   Dietary Fiber: 0g   Net Carbohydrates: 0g

CREAMY
COCONUT FUDG

Serves	: 12
Preparation time	: 20 minutes
Cooking time	: None
Freezing time	: 2 hours

ADDITIONAL TIP
You can also make these into balls but squares are much more convenient.

INGREDIENTS:

- 2 cups coconut oil
- ½ cup coconut cream
- ½ cup dark cocoa powder
- ¼ cup chopped almonds
- ¼ cup shredded coconut
- 1 teaspoon almond extract
- A pinch of salt
- Stevia to taste

DIRECTIONS:

1. Pour coconut cream and coconut oil into a large bowl and whisk using an electric beater. Stop when the mixture becomes smooth and glossy.

2. Slowly begin to add cocoa powder while continuing to mix. Make sure that there are no lumps.

3. Add in the rest of the ingredients.

4. Pour into a bread pan lined with parchment paper and freeze until set.

5. Cut into squares and enjoy!

NUTRITION FACTS (PER SERVING)

Calories: 172   Fat: 20g Protein: 0g   Total Carbohydrates: 1g   Dietary Fiber: 1g   Net Carbohydrates: 0g

NUTMEG NOUGATS

Serves : 12
Preparation time : 10 minutes
Cooking time : 5 minutes
Freezing time : 30 minutes

ADDITIONAL TIP
You can also coat them in cocoa powder instead.

INGREDIENTS:

- 1 cup cashew butter
- 1 cup heavy cream
- 1 cup shredded coconut
- 1 teaspoon vanilla extract
- ½ teaspoon ground nutmeg
- Stevia to taste

DIRECTIONS:

1. Melt the cashew butter over a double boiler.
2. Stir in dairy cream, vanilla extract, nutmeg and Stevia.
3. Remove from heat and allow to cool down a little.
4. Place in the refrigerator for at least half an hour.
5. Remove from the fridge and shape into small balls.
6. Coat with shredded coconut and chill for 2 hours. Then serve.

NUTRITION FACTS (PER SERVING)

Calories: 341   Fat: 34g   Protein: 3g   Total Carbohydrates: 13g   Dietary Fiber: 8g   Net Carbohydrates: 5g

COCOA BROWNIES

Serves : 12
Preparation time : 15 minutes
Cooking time : 25 minutes
Freezing time : None

ADDITIONAL TIP
Make brownie à la mode by serving with a scoop of keto ice cream.

INGREDIENTS:

- 1 egg
- ⅓ cup heavy cream
- ¾ cup almond butter
- ¼ cup cocoa powder
- 2 tablespoons grass-fed butter
- 2 teaspoon vanilla extract
- ¼ teaspoon baking powder
- A pinch of salt

DIRECTIONS:

1. Break the egg and whisk until smooth.

2. Add in all the wet ingredients and mix well.

3. Mix all the dry ingredients and sift them into the wet ingredients to make a batter.

4. Pour into a greased baking pan and bake for 25 minutes at 350°F or until a toothpick inserted in the middle comes out clean.

5. Cool, slice and serve.

NUTRITION FACTS (PER SERVING)

Calories: 184   Fat: 20g   Protein: 1g   Total Carbohydrates: 1g   Dietary Fiber: 0g   Net Carbohydrates: 1g

ORANGE OODLES

Serves	: 12
Preparation time	: 10 minutes
Cooking time	: None
Freezing time	: 2 hours

ADDITIONAL TIP

These are a versatile recipe. Try a variety of garnishes / additions. Some suggestions: toasted chopped nuts, shredded coconut, (more) cocoa powder

INGREDIENTS:

- 10 ounces coconut oil
- 4 tablespoons cocoa powder
- ¼ teaspoon blood orange extract
- Stevia to taste

DIRECTIONS:

1. Melt half the coconut oil over a double boiler and add in Stevia and orange extract.

2. Pour this mixture into candy molds, filling halfway.

3. Refrigerate until set.

4. In the meantime, melt the remaining coconut oil and stir in the cocoa powder and some Stevia. Make sure that there are no lumps.

5. Pour this into the molds, filling them up.

6. Return to your fridge and chill until completely set.

NUTRITION FACTS (PER SERVING)

Calories: 188   Fat: 21g   Protein: 1g   Total Carbohydrates: 1g   Dietary Fiber: 0g   Net Carbohydrates: 1g

MINI
MINTY HAPPINESS

Serves : 12   Preparation time : 45 minutes   Cooking time : None   Freezing time : 2 hours

INGREDIENTS:

- 1 ½ cups coconut oil
- 1 ¼ cups sunflower seed butter
- 1 cup dark chocolate chips (sugar free)
- ½ cup dried parsley
- 2 teaspoons vanilla extract
- 1 teaspoon peppermint extract
- A pinch of salt
- Stevia to taste

DIRECTIONS:

1. Melt together dark chocolate chips and coconut oil over a double boiler.

2. Add all the ingredients to a food processor and pulse until smooth.

3. Pour into round molds and freeze.

ADDITIONAL TIP
Add in some chopped dried cherries to make this even more festive

NUTRITION FACTS (PER SERVING)

Calories: 251   Fat: 25g   Protein: 3g   Total Carbohydrates: 7g   Dietary Fiber: 1g   Net Carbohydrates: 6g

CHEDDAR
CUPCAKE

Serves : 1   Preparation time : 5 minutes   Cooking time : 1 minutes   Freezing time : None

INGREDIENTS:

- 2 tablespoons shredded cheddar cheese
- 2 tablespoons grass-fed butter
- 3 tablespoons almond meal
- 1 tablespoons chopped green chilies
- ½ teaspoon baking powder
- ¼ teaspoon cayenne pepper
- 1 egg
- A pinch of salt

DIRECTIONS:

1. Whisk the egg until smooth. Add to a coffee mug.

2. Mix the cheese and softened butter. Add in the rest of the ingredients. Mix well.

3. Add to the egg and mix well.

4. Microwave for 1 minute or until a toothpick inserted in the center comes out clean.

5. Eat straight from the mug.

NUTRITION FACTS (PER SERVING)

Calories: 492   Fat: 49g   Protein: 18g   Total Carbohydrates: 6g   Dietary Fiber: 3g   Net Carbohydrates: 3g

SEED-FILLED BOMBS

Serves : 12
Preparation time : 35 minutes
Cooking time : None
Freezing time : 1 hours

ADDITIONAL TIP
You can add any combination of seeds that you like. I like making a nice colorful mixture

INGREDIENTS:

- ⅔ cup coconut butter
- 2 ½ tablespoons coconut oil
- 2 tablespoons cacao powder
- 1 tablespoon hemp seeds
- 1 tablespoon flaxseeds
- 1 tablespoon chia seeds
- 1 tablespoon pumpkin seeds
- 1 teaspoon vanilla extract
- Stevia to taste

DIRECTIONS:

1. Melt coconut butter and coconut oil over a double boiler.

2. Combine all the ingredients and pour into molds.

3. Refrigerate until they are semi-set and doughy. Keep stored in the fridge for further use.

NUTRITION FACTS (PER SERVING)

Calories: 121   Fat: 11g   Protein: 2g   Total Carbohydrates: 4g   Dietary Fiber: 3g   Net Carbohydrates: 1g

NUTTY GINGER BOMBS

Serves	: 12
Preparation time	: 5 minutes
Cooking time	: None
Freezing time	: 2 hours

ADDITIONAL TIP
Fresh ginger works best but if you don't have access to it, you can also use ground ginger

INGREDIENTS:

- 4 ounces shredded coconut
- 2 ounces grass-fed butter
- 2 ounces coconut oil
- 1 tablespoon grated ginger
- 1 teaspoon ground cinnamon
- 1 teaspoon vanilla extract
- ½ tablespoon crushed roasted cashews
- Stevia to taste
- A pinch of salt

DIRECTIONS:

1. Soften the butter and coconut oil.
2. Combine all the ingredients.
3. Pour into molds and freeze.

NUTRITION FACTS (PER SERVING)

Calories: 79   Fat: 9g   Protein: 0g   Total Carbohydrates: 1g   Dietary Fiber: 0g   Net Carbohydrates: 1g

CUSTARD CUPS

Serves : 12   Preparation time : 5 minutes   Cooking time : None   Freezing time : 40 minutes

INGREDIENTS:

- ½ pound grass-fed butter
- 2 cups coconut milk
- ½ cup coconut oil
- ½ cup shredded coconut
- ¼ cup protein powder (any flavor of your preference)
- 2 tablespoons gelatin
- 1 ½ teaspoons vanilla extract
- 6 teaspoons xylitol
- 5 egg yolks
- Stevia to taste

DIRECTIONS:

1. Beat the egg yolks until smooth and creamy.

2. Melt together butter and coconut oil in a saucepan. Add coconut milk to the mixture.

3. Add gelatin and keep stirring until gelatin dissolves and the mixture begins to thicken a little.

4. Remove from heat and allow to cool. Stir in protein powder and vanilla extract.

5. Pour into bowls and sprinkle shredded coconut on top.

6. Chill before serving.

ADDITIONAL TIP
You can make varying flavors by using different flavored protein powders.

NUTRITION FACTS (PER SERVING)

Calories: 349   Fat: 37g   Protein: 2g   Total Carbohydrates: 5g   Dietary Fiber: 1g   Net Carbohydrates: 4g

NUTTY
WHITE CHOCOLATE

Serves	: 12
Preparation time	: 5 minutes
Cooking time	: None
Freezing time	: 1-2 hours

ADDITIONAL TIP
Granulated Stevia is optional. You can also sprinkle with some cocoa powder or shredded coconut.

INGREDIENTS:

- ½ cup chopped roasted pecans
- 4 tablespoons cocoa butter
- 4 tablespoons coconut butter
- 4 tablespoons coconut oil
- 1 teaspoon scraped vanilla bean
- Granulated and liquid Stevia to taste
- A pinch of salt

DIRECTIONS:

1. Combine all the ingredients to form a batter.

2. Pour into a bread pan lined with parchment paper.

3. Freeze until set.

4. Cut into squares and sprinkle with some granulated Stevia.

NUTRITION FACTS (PER SERVING)

Calories: 92   Fat: 10g   Protein: 0g   Total Carbohydrates: 1g   Dietary Fiber: 0g   Net Carbohydrates: 1g

FLUFFY
FAT BOMBS

Serves : 12   Preparation time : 10 minutes   Cooking time : 6 minutes   Freezing time : 1 hour

INGREDIENTS:

- 2 cups heavy cream
- ⅔ cup sour cream
- 2 teaspoons ground cinnamon
- 1 teaspoon scraped vanilla bean
- ¼ teaspoon ground cardamom
- 4 egg yolks
- Stevia to taste

DIRECTIONS:

1. Whisk egg yolks in a glass bowl until smooth and creamy.

2. Place the bowl over a double boiler and add in rest of the ingredients.

3. Remove from heat and cool to room temperature.

4. Refrigerate for about an hour and then whisk.

5. Pour into molds and freeze.

ADDITIONAL TIP
You can also add in some cocoa powder.

NUTRITION FACTS (PER SERVING)

Calories: 363   Fat: 40g   Protein: 2g   Total Carbohydrates: 1g   Dietary Fiber: 0g   Net Carbohydrates: 1g

CHEESE-CENTERED BACON BALLS

Serves   : 35-40
Preparation time : 3 minutes
Cooking time   : 5 minutes
Freezing time   : None

INGREDIENTS:

- 35-40 slices bacon
- 16 ounces shredded mozzarella cheese
- 8 tablespoons grass-fed butter
- 8 tablespoons almond flour
- 6 tablespoons psyllium husk powder
- ¼ teaspoon onion powder
- ¼ teaspoon garlic powder
- 1 egg
- 2 cups clarified butter (or ghee or oil)
- Salt and pepper to taste

ADDITIONAL TIP
This does take a little bit of time as the wrapping process can be slow and tedious so plan ahead.

DIRECTIONS:

1. Prepare a double boiler.
2. Melt butter and add in half the mozzarella cheese. Wait for it to become gooey and sticky.
3. Add in the egg and beat with a fork until all is smooth.
4. Add in rest of the ingredients, minus the bacon and remaining cheese, and mix well. Remove from heat.
5. At this point it will have a thick, dough-like consistency. Allow to cool and then roll out into a flat triangular shape.
6. Spread the remaining cheese on half of the dough and then fold it over, like a sandwich with cheese in the middle.
7. Fold it over once more and seal the edges using your hands.
8. Cut into small squares, you'll get about 35-40.
9. Wrap a slice of bacon around each piece and secure with a toothpick. Repeat for all.
10. Heat oil/ghee in a deep pot and deep fry until brown and crispy.
11. Serve straight away.

NUTRITION FACTS (PER SERVING)

Calories: 275   Fat: 31g   Protein: 0g   Total Carbohydrates: 2g   Dietary Fiber: 1g   Net Carbohydrates: 1g

You May Also Like

Please visit the below link for other books by the author

http://ketojane.com/books

Made in the USA
Middletown, DE
23 June 2019